CYBERSECURITY

Right Access at the Right Time

Avinash Majeti

Contents

Chapter 1: Introduction

Security is the fundamental necessity required to safeguard an organization. Every industry, digital, financial and physical asset requires security. To safeguard an asset means to protect it from future vulnerability. The foundation of every industry, process, website and practice; is security. Securing an asset means providing safety features to a valuable item or asset; such items can be classified as information, monetary and financial assets, and digital assets. Cybersecurity is the protection of digital information and assets. Before diving into the world of cybersecurity, let us first understand the concept of security.

Security, Cybersecurity and its Foundational Model

As discussed earlier, security means to protect assets from harm and prevent unauthorized use. In the world of software engineering, Cybersecurity is the practice of protecting computers, networks, programs and data from digital threats. It utilizes all measures taken to defend against malicious attacks, from different types of malware and ransomware to phishing and hacking that aim to access private information, alter, or destroy sensitive information.

In other words, cybersecurity ensures that only legitimate users and processes can reach data or systems, preserving the CIA triad: The three foundational core principles in Cybersecurity are called the CIA Triad, Confidentiality, Integrity and Availability. These principles are the core practices a security analyst must follow to ensure proper safeguarding of digital assets from outwardly attacks.

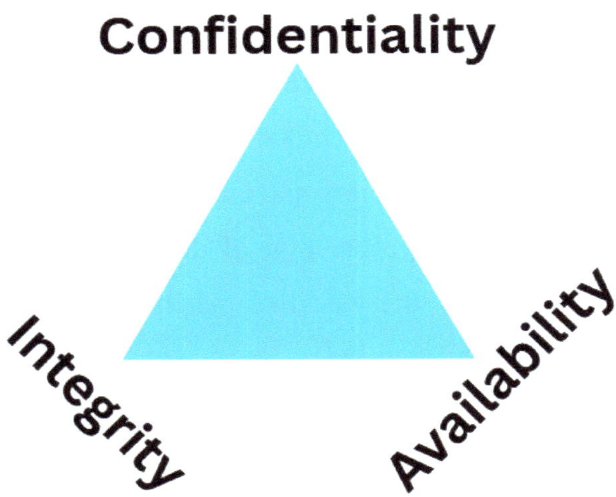

CIA Triad:

1. **Confidentiality:** Confidentiality ensures that data and sensitive information are protected from unauthorized access. It involves utilizing safeguarding measures such as encryption, access

controls and **data masking**.

2. **Integrity:** Integrity ensures that information provided to users is accurate, complete and from a trusted source. It involves preventing unauthorized modification or destruction of data and maintaining its authenticity. Utilizing measures such as digital signatures to ensure that information is complete and unedited.

3. **Availability:** The availability principle ensures that only users with authorized access have complete timely and reliable access to information and data. Ensuring availability involves utilizing measures such as recovery planning and fast connections to provide quick access of information for users.

Effective cybersecurity practices utilize a multi layered approach. Organizations deploy multiple protective technologies such as firewalls, encryption, and identity controls. These layers are coordinated with processes and policies so that they complement each other. For instance, one layer might block known **malware**, another might encrypt data, and yet another enforces access controls. Together, people, processes and technology form a strategy that can detect, repel and recover from cyberattacks.

Role of Cybersecurity Professionals

Organizations employ dedicated experts called security analysts, engineers and administrators, whose main objective is to protect the digital environment. These professionals design and implement security controls, monitor systems for suspicious activity, and respond to incidents. In other words, they work on the "front lines" against cyber threats. At a high level, security teams ensure that networks, servers, devices and data remain safe. They configure firewalls, manage identity tools, analyze logs, and quickly address breaches or vulnerabilities. By doing so, they safeguard an organization's digital well-being and keep its information assets resilient against evolving attacks. In essence, cybersecurity professionals keep digital resources safe and reliable under all conditions.

Chapter 2: Introduction to Identity Management: The 3 A's of IAM

Today's cyber environment is a highly complex, enterprise-based network that harbors thousands of employees, business owners and customers and countless devices, all accessing servers and multiple cloud services. Each person requires a device, which in turn needs a digital identity, and many logins occur from different locations and networks. This explosion of identities has attracted attackers' attention. IBM X-Force's annual Threat Intelligence Index report found valid account compromises accounted for almost **one-third of global cyberattacks** last year, making it the most-common initial access vector for attacks in 2023 . In other words, as networks grow and fragment, a robust IAM has become a necessary component of Cybersecurity.

What is IAM?

Identity and Access Management (IAM) is the cybersecurity discipline for managing user identities and their access rights within an IT system. In practice, IAM covers creating and deleting digital identities, assigning permissions, and enforcing who can access what. T he goal is to ensure that "the right people can access the right resources for the right reasons at the right time". This means users are verified and granted only the privileges they require, exactly when they need them. IAM has become critical in modern networks, especially with cloud services, remote work, and automated systems increasing the number of identities, so organizations can prevent unauthorized access while enabling productivity.

The "Three A's" of IAM.

IAM is often summarized by the 3 A's: Authentication, Authorization and Audit. Authentication verifies that a user is who they claim to be. Authorization determines what that verified user is allowed to do. Audit (or Accounting) involves logging and reviewing those user actions. Together these three pillars form the core of identity security: first authenticate the user, then authorize appropriate access, and finally monitor what occurs in a digital environment.

Authentication

Authentication is the process of **verifying identity**. Users (or devices) must prove they are who they claim to be before gaining any access. Typically this is done by presenting one or more *authentication factors*, for example, something you know (a password or PIN), something you have (a security token or smart card), or something you are (a fingerprint, facial scan, or other biometric). Modern IAM systems often use a combination of factors (MFA) for stronger security. For instance, a user might enter a password and then confirm a code sent to their phone. When the presented credentials match the stored identity profile, the system grants access.

Common authentication methods include:

- **Passwords/PINs:** The most basic method. Passwords are easy for users to employ but notoriously vulnerable. Attackers use brute force, phishing or credential stuffing to crack them. However, relying solely on passwords is "one of the weakest" forms of authentication.
- **Security Tokens/Keys:** Physical devices or software tokens generate time-based codes or store cryptographic keys. For example, an app or hardware token that displays a rotating code is a common second factor. These are more secure than passwords alone, but devices can be lost or stolen, so they require careful provisioning and backup procedures.
- **Digital Certificates:** Public-key certificates issued by a certificate authority authenticate machines or software. This uses encryption under the hood, possession of the private key proves identity. Certificates are very strong when properly

managed, but they introduce complexity.

- **Biometrics:** Unique human traits like fingerprints, facial recognition or iris scans. Biometrics tie identity to a physical person and can't be forgotten. However, they raise privacy concerns and in rare cases can be spoofed. Also, if a biometric template is compromised, it can't be "changed" like a password.

- **Multi-Factor Authentication (MFA):** Combines two or more methods above. For example, a password plus a one-time code or fingerprint. MFA is one of the most effective defenses against many attacks. It greatly reduces risk, though it requires extra user effort and system support.

Each method has trade-offs: passwords are familiar but weak; tokens and certificates are strong but require management; biometrics are convenient but sensitive. A layered approach such as using password and tokens is generally recommended to balance convenience and security.

Authorization

Authorization determines what an authenticated user is allowed to do, in other words, what resources or actions their identity permits. Once a user's identity is confirmed via authentication, the IAM system checks the user's assigned privileges and enforces access policies. This can be role-based

(RBAC) or attribute-based (ABAC), etc. In RBAC, for example, permissions are tied to a user's job function: a developer role might grant access to code repositories but not to payroll systems. The IAM engine looks up the user's role and then authorizes only the actions or data that the role allows.

A fundamental concept in authorization is the **principle of least privilege**. This means every user (and process) is given the minimum set of rights needed to perform their job, and nothing more. For instance, a junior analyst might have "read-only" access to certain logs, whereas a senior engineer might have "modify" rights. Over-provisioning (granting excess rights) is explicitly avoided. Proper authorization prevents scope creep: even if an attacker steals an account, they can only use the permissions of that account. By enforcing fine-grained access policies and promptly revoking unneeded rights, IAM ensures that users can only perform authorized actions. In practice, authorization policies and enforced by access-control systems ensure that every request is matched against the user's allowed privileges.

Audit (Logging and Compliance)

Audit in IAM refers to **monitoring and recording** user access and activity. Every time a user authenticates or accesses a resource, an entry should be logged. The IAM system tracks who accessed what and when. These logs serve two key purposes:

security and compliance. From a security perspective, auditing helps detect anomalies, for example, an unusual login time or access from a new location may trigger an alert. Auditing "ensures that nobody (including malicious insiders) has access they shouldn't" by reviewing logged actions.

From a compliance standpoint, many regulations mandate strict access controls and audit trails. For example, laws like GDPR (data protection), SOX (financial reporting) and HIPAA (healthcare privacy) require organizations to implement and document controls over who can see or modify sensitive data. IAM auditing helps meet these rules. Specifically, regulations often demand regular reviews of access rights and a record of all privileged actions. If an organization can show an audit trail (who accessed a record and when), it can prove compliance or quickly investigate a suspected breach.

Right Access at the Right Time

A key principle of IAM is granting precise access only when needed. IAM exists to give "the right people" exactly the access they need "for the right reasons at the right time". In practice, this means enforcing least privilege: users get the minimum permissions required for their role. For example, an employee who only needs to read reports should not have permission to alter them. Access can also be time-bound or just-in-time, so that elevated rights are revoked as soon as a task is done. By tightly aligning access with actual need, IAM minimizes unnecessary exposure: resources stay locked down except during legitimate use. This fine-grained control, limiting privileges and verifying requests, is crucial to preventing misuse and enforcing policy.

Chapter 3: Identity Lifecycle Management

In the world of cybersecurity, identity lifecycle management (ILM) refers to the set of processes governing a user's digital identity from the moment they join an organization, through role changes, to the point they leave. ILM is a critical component of Identity and Access Management (IAM) and ensures that access rights are continuously aligned with users' current roles and statuses.

Without strong lifecycle management, organizations risk overprovisioning, account misuse, and dangerous gaps in security, especially with high employee turnover and hybrid work environments.

Joiners: Provisioning New Users

The joiner phase refers to onboarding new employees, contractors, or third-party users. As soon as someone joins an organization, their identity must be established and recorded in a central directory. This involves assigning a unique user ID, generating credentials, and provisioning accounts for required systems, applications, and networks.

Provisioning is ideally automated through IAM tools that apply standardized role templates, reducing the risk of manual errors or inconsistent privileges. For example, a new marketing employee may automatically receive access to email, CRM tools, and shared drives specific to their team.

Missteps in this phase, such as assigning administrative rights to a regular employee or failing to enforce multifactor authentication (MFA) can result in vulnerabilities from day one.

Movers: Role Changes and Access Adjustments

In most organizations, employees do not remain in a single role indefinitely. Promotions, lateral transfers, and temporary assignments all trigger changes in access needs. This mover phase is often where IAM systems fail if not tightly integrated with HR systems and workflows.

For example, an engineer who becomes a team lead may need access to budget dashboards but no longer requires hands-on access to production systems. If their previous rights aren't revoked during the role transition, they may retain excess privileges, increasing the attack surface.

This phenomenon, also known as a **privilege creep** is considered to be a huge risk, as users accumulate unnecessary access over time. Gartner has emphasized the importance of real-time access adjustment, stating that identity governance should be dynamic and responsive to business changes to reduce security exposure (Gartner IAM Summit, 2023).

Proper lifecycle management ensures access changes are tightly coupled with HR events, and that every role change prompts a reassessment of privileges. Many IAM systems support "re-certification" or access reviews during role transitions to verify that only appropriate permissions remain.

Leavers: De-provisioning Users

When users leave an organization, whether due to resignation, termination, or contract expiration, it is imperative to immediately revoke access to all accounts and systems. Delays in de-provisioning can result in **orphaned accounts**, which are user profiles that remain active despite the user's departure.

De-provisioning involves:

- Disabling all user credentials
- Revoking session tokens or API keys
- Removing the user from distribution lists, groups, or team spaces

- Archiving email or files as needed for compliance
- Notifying system owners to validate final actions

IAM systems can automate much of this process, ensuring that exit procedures are triggered as soon as HR marks the user's status as inactive.

The Cost of Orphaned Accounts

Orphaned accounts are those that persist after the user has left, these are a silent but dangerous threat. Attackers target these accounts because they are often unmonitored yet may retain powerful privileges. A compromised orphan account can act as a backdoor into sensitive systems, especially if MFA is not enforced or logging is disabled.

Real-World Failures and Lessons

- **Target Data Breach (2013):** Hackers infiltrated Target's systems using credentials from a third-party HVAC vendor. The vendor's credentials weren't adequately scoped or time-bound, allowing lateral movement across the network. Better lifecycle and access controls could have prevented the breach.
- **Capital One Breach (2019):** A former employee exploited excessive permissions on an orphaned AWS role. The role hadn't been reviewed or de-provisioned properly, giving

unauthorized access to over 100 million customer records. IAM lifecycle gaps were a key root cause.

- **GitHub Access Mismanagement (2022):** A study by GitGuardian found thousands of stale access tokens left in repositories. Many belonged to former contributors whose access was never revoked—a clear lifecycle management failure.

These examples demonstrate that every stage in the identity lifecycle carries risk. Without well-defined provisioning, access adjustments, and de-provisioning workflows, even a single overlooked account can result in catastrophic loss.

Chapter 4:
Access Reviews and Role-Based Access Control (RBAC)

Understanding Access Reviews

Access reviews are a systematic process of validating who has access to which resources, why they have it, and whether that access is still justified. Over time, users accumulate permissions due to changing roles, project-based assignments, or errors in provisioning. Without routine evaluations, this accumulation leads to **privilege creep**—a major security vulnerability.

These reviews help prevent unauthorized access, ensure regulatory compliance, and maintain alignment with the principle of least privilege. They also support cleaner IAM governance and reduce clutter in access configurations.

Why Reviews Are Necessary

Access control is not a one-time setup. In dynamic organizations, user roles change frequently—employees are promoted, reassigned, or offboarded. In each of these scenarios, permissions need to be updated.

Access reviews fill this gap by enabling organizations to routinely audit user permissions. Without them, there is a high risk of over-provisioning, orphaned accounts, and untracked administrative access. Gartner has repeatedly emphasized that identity-related risks are among the most under-monitored aspects of enterprise security.

Types of Access Reviews

1. Periodic Access Reviews: These occur at scheduled intervals—monthly, quarterly, or annually. Typically aligned with compliance cycles, they are useful for producing auditable trails of access decisions. However, the effectiveness of periodic reviews can degrade if they become a “check-the-box” routine rather than a genuine assessment.

2. Continuous or Real-Time Access Reviews: Powered by automation and analytics, these reviews happen dynamically. For instance, if an employee hasn't accessed a particular system in 90 days, their access may be automatically flagged for revocation or verification.

Continuous reviews reduce the risk window by catching anomalies as they occur rather than waiting for the next scheduled cycle.

Who Should Conduct Reviews?

Access reviews are collaborative. No single person has all the context needed to assess access across the board. Responsibility typically breaks down as follows:

- **Line Managers:** Understand what their team members do daily. They are best placed to confirm whether permissions align with responsibilities.
- **Application Owners:** Know the sensitivity and function of systems. They can decide whether a user should retain access based on business needs.
- **Compliance Teams:** Ensure that reviews follow regulatory standards and are properly documented.

Each of these stakeholders must participate to ensure access is appropriate, justified, and transparent.

Review Best Practices

To maximize efficiency and accuracy, the following best practices are widely recommended:

- **Policy-Driven Reviews:** Establish triggers (e.g., role changes, inactivity, project end) to initiate access review workflows.
- **Risk-Based Prioritization:** Focus reviews on high-risk

assets or users (e.g., privileged accounts, financial systems).

- **Automation:** IAM platforms should generate user-role-resource matrices, send notifications, and revoke access based on outcomes.
- **Certification Workflows:** Every review should result in a certification, with decisions recorded and auditable.
- **User Attestation:** In some cases, users themselves can attest whether they still need access—especially for generic or shared resources.

Integrating with Compliance Frameworks

Access reviews are a staple requirement for compliance with most global security and privacy frameworks:

- **SOX** demands strict controls on who can access financial systems.
- **HIPAA** requires regular audits of access to health records.
- **GDPR** emphasizes transparency and control over personal data access.
- **ISO 27001** includes periodic review of information access rights as a key control.

Auditors often request logs or proof that access was reviewed and certified. IAM tools can automate the generation of such reports, linking reviews to tickets or digital signatures to create clear audit trails.

Role-Based Access Control (RBAC)

How RBAC Works

RBAC assigns access based on roles within an organization. Rather than manually assigning permissions to every user, administrators define roles—such as "Finance Analyst," "HR Manager," or "IT Admin"—and assign those roles to users. Each role bundles together the permissions required for a specific job function.

This structure simplifies access management, improves consistency, and enforces the **principle of least privilege** by design.

Benefits of RBAC

- **Scalability:** Easy to manage for large organizations.
- **Auditability:** Roles are clearly documented, making it easier to verify access.
- **Consistency:** New users receive access based on their roles, minimizing errors.

Role Engineering and Role Mining

Role engineering is the process of designing and refining roles. It often begins with **role mining**—analyzing current user access patterns to identify logical groupings.

Roles should be named logically and hierarchically, e.g., "Sales.Basic," "Sales.Manager," and "Sales.Admin." Over time, role structures should be refined based on access usage trends and organizational changes.

RBAC vs ABAC vs PBAC

Model	Description	Best Used For
RBAC	Roles assigned based on job functions	Stable Organizational structures
ABAC	Access Is based on Attributes, eg departments, locations	Dynamic Environments
PBAC	Policy driven access based on logic and context	Advanced Adaptive access decisions

Many organizations now use **hybrid models**, combining RBAC for broad access and ABAC/PBAC for granular, dynamic controls.

Challenges of RBAC

Although Role Based Access Control helps an organization get ahead in compartmentalization and diverting necessary resources in role management. Each and every cybersecurity based practice has its own sets of unique rules and methods and thus this practice also comes with its own set of unique challenges.

- **Role Explosion:** Too many roles make the system complex and hard to manage.
- **Static Nature:** RBAC cannot adapt easily to temporary needs or contextual factors.
- **Initial Design Overhead:** Defining effective roles takes time and cross-department collaboration.

Nonetheless, RBAC remains the backbone of access control for most medium-to-large organizations.

Practical RBAC Implementation Steps

1. **Inventory Permissions:** Document all existing access points.
2. **Analyze Access Patterns:** Use IAM tools to identify clusters of common access.
3. **Design Roles:** Align roles with job functions.
4. **Assign Users:** Map users to appropriate roles.

5. **Review Regularly:** Adjust roles based on feedback, audits, and business changes.
6. **Automate Lifecycle Events:** Ensure joiners, movers, and leavers are handled automatically via HR/IAM integrations.

Chapter 5: IAM Trends and the Future

Identity and Access Management (IAM) continues to evolve rapidly as organizations adapt to new technologies and changing threat landscapes. In this chapter we explore emerging trends shaping IAM and look ahead to how they will influence security in the coming years. We discuss how Zero Trust architecture is tightly bound to IAM, why identity has replaced the traditional network perimeter, and how artificial intelligence and machine learning are reshaping access governance. We also examine additional trends, like passwordless authentication, decentralized identity, cloud identity orchestration, and the growth of device identities, that are redefining the way we think about access.

Zero Trust and IAM

Zero Trust has become a guiding paradigm for cybersecurity, and identity management lies at its core. In a Zero Trust model, no user or device is trusted by default simply because it's on a certain network; every access attempt must be explicitly verified. This principle aligns perfectly with IAM's mission of "never trust, always verify," relying on strong authentication, precise authorization, and continual monitoring. For example, the Cloud Security Alliance notes that Zero Trust "requires implementing strong authentication (MFA, cryptography) and access controls (least privilege, RBAC, ABAC, P BAC)". In practice this means multi-factor authentication, user and device attestation, microsegmented access, and continuous re-checking of each user's rights.

IAM also plays a crucial role in eliminating hidden risks often called "shadow access." Under strict Zero Trust thinking, no implicit permissions should exist. As CSA emphasizes, in a true Zero Trust environment "no access should be granted implicitly or by default", every permission must be explicitly and intentionally given. This principle forces organizations to continuously audit and prune entitlements. Not coincidentally, U.S. federal Zero Trust guidelines actually highlight identity as a foundational pillar: CISA's Zero Trust Maturity Model calls for "maturing capabilities in the Identity...pillar" as the basis for enterprise transition to ZTA. In other words, government policy underscores that IAM improvements (like phishing-resistant MFA and tight privilege controls) are the first step toward Zero Trust.

Looking ahead, Zero Trust and IAM will continue to reinforce each other. As more organizations adopt Zero Trust, they will invest heavily in IAM technologies, for instance, rolling out continuous behavioral analytics, just-in-time access, and adaptive policies. Conversely, as IAM platforms become more sophisticated (supporting real-time risk scoring and context-aware access), they enable even tighter Zero Trust enforcement. This interplay means security teams must consider Zero Trust and IAM side by side. In effect, we argue that IAM investments are now synonymous with Zero Trust projects: modernizing IAM is essentially the Zero Trust journey.

Identity as the New Perimeter

With the shift away from fixed network boundaries, identity has effectively become today's perimeter for security. In the early enterprise era, firewalls and VPNs defined the edge and assumed internal users were trusted. But as cloud services and remote work dominate, that castle-and-moat model no longer holds. In fact, one industry analyst writes that "the old perimeter is gone… In its place, identity has emerged to enable users to gain access to resources". In practical terms, employees and devices can log in from anywhere, so the key question is always "who is this?" rather than "where did they come from?"

Identity has essentially "replaced network boundaries as today's security perimeter". Authentication and user credentials are now the first line of defense, not source IPs or office locations. In this identity-defined perimeter, access controls like multi-factor authentication (MFA) and single sign-on become the new "firewalls." Importantly, identity is now the core attack surface for adversaries. Identity is literally "the key to unlocking access," and today it is "the core attack surface" that hackers go after. Attackers know that compromising a user's login credentials often provides entry to systems without needing to bypass a network wall.

This shift has broad implications. Organizations must pivot from network-centric monitoring to identity-centric monitoring. Security analytics and policies increasingly focus on who the user (or device) is, what roles they have, and how they behave, rather than just on IP addresses or network zones. Strengthening IAM (for example, by adding step-up authentication for sensitive tasks or by quickly revoking access when devices are lost) directly hardens what is now the "perimeter" of the enterprise. In many ways, our industry has shifted from defending buildings to protecting identities. The practical result is that every IAM improvement, from tighter access reviews to stronger login safeguards, now translates directly into better perimeter security.

AI and Machine Learning in Access Governance

Artificial intelligence and machine learning (AI/ML) are playing an increasingly important role in IAM, especially in governance, monitoring, and automation. In a large modern enterprise, simply managing who has access to hundreds or thousands of apps and services is a massive data problem. AI and ML help by detecting patterns and anomalies in this sea of identity data that human administrators would miss. For instance, many IAM platforms now incorporate ML-based engines that learn normal user behavior (usual login times, device usage, access patterns) and then flag anything unusual. Industry sources highlight that ML algorithms can "detect suspicious activities, such as unauthorized access attempts or abnormal usage patterns". In practice, this means outlier logins or privilege escalations can be spotted instantly, if an account suddenly logs in from a new country or starts requesting sensitive files, AI can identify that as high risk in real time.

Beyond threat detection, AI is also used to streamline IAM processes. Many vendors now offer identity threat detection and response (ITDR) tools that continuously scan for compromised or risky credentials. Similarly, AI can assist in identity governance: by analyzing how users consume resources, machine learning can suggest how to group permissions into roles or flag accounts that have too many rights. For example, a machine learning model might notice that only a few finance team members ever open certain transaction reports, it can then recommend refining access so only those roles have that capability. This kind of role mining accelerates the tedious task of access certification and helps enforce least privilege.

AI is also automating routine tasks in IAM. Common

activities like provisioning a new employee's accounts, deprovisioning departed staff, or even generating access review reports can be partially handled by AI-based workflows. For instance, new tools allow administrators to ask a chatbot "who currently has access to the payroll system?" and receive answers generated from the IAM database. Even more advanced, administrators can use AI assistants to offload tasks: a system might automatically create and assign a temporary credential for a contractor, or automatically revoking access when a user's role changes.

Generative AI has also started to get into the security fields. Although it had entered the IAM space a long time ago, it still brings out unique breakthroughs that efficiently improves security and role management. For example, one could imagine a GenAI assistant that examines an IAM deployment and recommends improvements or writes audit summaries. In theory, GenAI might even predict which identities are likely targets by learning from attack trends. Of course, these applications come with caveats: training data quality and privacy must be managed carefully. But the trajectory is clear: advanced AI will provide more proactive recommendations in IAM.

Overall, AI and ML are transforming IAM from static, manual processes into adaptive, intelligence-driven ones. The chief benefit is speed and scale: AI can spot and respond to identity risks in near real-time, whereas humans typically audit identity policies infrequently. In short, AI-powered analytics and automation make identity governance continuously responsive, discovering compromised accounts, recommending policy changes, or even taking automated actions, in ways traditional tools could not.

Cloud, Multi-Cloud, and Hybrid IAM

The rapid rise of cloud computing and distributed workforces has dramatically complicated IAM. Few organizations today are "all on-premises", most have a mix of on-prem apps, private cloud, multiple public clouds (AWS, Azure, GCP), and a variety of SaaS services. This hybrid/multi-cloud reality often leads to "identity sprawl": different usernames and credentials for different environments, inconsistent policies, and gaps in visibility. For example, an employee might use Active Directory to log into their Windows PC, but log into G Suite with a Google account, and use Okta to access Salesforce. Coordinating these disparate systems is a major challenge.

A recent industry survey underscored this pain: the Cloud Security Alliance found that 71% of enterprises struggle to enforce modern SSO and MFA on their legacy applications. In response, a new concept known as the "identity fabric" (or identity orchestration) has emerged. The identity fabric is essentially a unifying layer that connects all the disparate identity stores, on-prem directories, cloud IdPs, SaaS user directories, etc., and enforces consistent access policies across them. Using identity fabrics, a company can keep its existing Active Directory and cloud identities, but still tie them together under one policy engine.

In practice, identity fabric platforms or orchestration tools offer features like directory bridging (syncing on-prem AD with Azure AD or Okta), policy-based connectors, and centralized dashboards. Many IAM vendors and startups now provide such solutions. The end goal is that an administrator defines a user's roles and access rights in one place, and the fabric distributes and enforces that across all cloud and on-premise apps. This approach enables a "best of both worlds" strategy: organizations can gradually move to cloud IAM (IDaaS) without ripping out every legacy system.

Hybrid IAM is especially important in scenarios like mergers and federal agencies. For example, U.S. government agencies under Zero Trust mandates are consolidating various identity systems onto shared platforms. In the private sector, a merger might be smoother if the two companies can federate identities instead of merging Active Directory forests overnight. Globally, we see similar patterns: major corporations and governments (in Europe, Asia, etc.) are building identity bridges to support cross-cloud operations. In the end, a robust cloud/hybrid IAM strategy should give the ability to treat all user identities, whether from Okta, Azure AD, Google Workspace, or a local LDAP, under one umbrella of governance.

Why IAM is Foundational

Through all these trends, one point is clear: IAM underpins almost every aspect of cybersecurity and digital transformation. It provides the essential foundation by controlling who (or what) has access to what resources. As one industry analysis put it, in 2025 IAM has "become a strategic pillar in enterprise security". We couldn't agree more. Without solid identity and access controls, every other security measure is weakened.

IAM is foundational for several reasons. First, it protects the keys to the kingdom. Nearly every significant data breach involves stolen, weak, or misused credentials. In other words, if an attacker can compromise an identity, they effectively bypass many defenses. A strong IAM program (with MFA, anomaly detection, and least-privilege policies) is thus the first line of defense against intrusion. An effective IAM system continuously searches out and removes excessive privileges; in fact, industry reports find that a large majority of organizations have many users with unnecessary access rights. Eliminating such over-privilege through IAM governance drastically shrinks the attack surface.

Second, IAM supports compliance and audit requirements. Laws and regulations like GDPR, HIPAA, and SOX all require that organizations track and control access to sensitive data. IAM systems provide the tools to record who accessed what and to enforce policies systematically. For example, with modern IAM and AI tools, a company can automatically generate a report of all users who accessed personal data over the last month, something that would be very difficult without centralized identity logs. In essence, IAM gives organizations the visibility and control needed to meet legal obligations and prove that access is appropriate.

Third, IAM enables agility and business innovation. Think of all the modern IT projects that rely on IAM: migrating to cloud apps, implementing mobile device management, merging companies, opening B2B portals, or moving to SaaS. Each of these initiatives depends on being able to trust and manage digital identities across contexts. For instance, enabling remote work securely is impossible without strong IAM (single sign-on, conditional access, etc.). Without IAM foundations, companies would have to reinvent authentication for every new service. By having a mature IAM platform, organizations can quickly onboard new systems and users without falling back to insecure shortcuts (like reusing default credentials or sharing accounts).

Finally, IAM builds trust. In a hybrid world, customers, partners, and employees expect seamless yet secure access. Consistent identity controls (SSO, MFA, user self-service, etc.) build confidence that the right people get the right access at the right time. IAM is the thread that ties together encryption, network security, data classification, and even physical access. When identity is managed properly, it anchors all these layers, from ensuring your bank app only opens for you, to letting an employee use one credential for multiple approved cloud services.

In summary, the trends we have examined all reinforce one conclusion: IAM is not optional but essential. From Zero Trust to AI-driven governance, from passwordless logins to device identity, every new security paradigm relies on strong identity management. Organizations that invest wisely in IAM, by adopting these trends thoughtfully, will be better positioned to ward off future threats and comply with evolving regulations. Those that neglect IAM will quickly find their network and data exposed, because in today's world an attacker only needs a single compromised identity to unravel most defenses. Identity is, and always will be, the foundation of security.

www.ingramcontent.com/pod-product-compliance
Lightning Source LLC
LaVergne TN
LVHW050924210926
848482LV00012B/533
* 9 7 9 8 3 3 0 3 9 0 2 8 1 *